50!

...Lessons on the Holy Spirit

Matt Friedeman

Teleios Press

Copyright © 2014 Teleios Press, Jackson, MS

Scriptures taken from the Holy Bible, New International Version®, NIV®
Copyright © 1973, 1978, 1984, 2011 by Biblica, Inc®
Used by permission. All rights reserved worldwide.

All rights reserved, unless otherwise stated in the text. No part of this book may be reproduced or transmitted in any form or by any means, electronic or mechanical, including photocopying, recording, or by any information storage or retrieval system, without permission in writing from the Publisher.

Printed in the United States of America

First edition 2014

TELEIOS PRESS

http://www.teleiospress.com

To the Phillips family:
David, Dana, Danae and Dawson...
DaySpring heroes!

"You shall count seven full weeks from the day after the Sabbath, from the day that you brought the sheaf of the wave offering. You shall county fifty days to the day after the seventh Sabbath…And you shall make a proclamation on the same day. You shall hold a holy convocation…"

Leviticus 23:15-16, 21
(God's announcement of
the festival of Pentecost)

Introduction

This booklet can be used individually for personal devotions and inspiration. But it was originally designed to help families and groups in the local church count up the days to Pentecost (the day including Easter for fifty days until the Sunday of Pentecost). On the previous page it is noted that in Leviticus, God ordained the date as a harvest festival. Many years later, after the resurrection of Jesus, God would use that date to birth the Church with the power of the Holy Spirit.

Many local churches do little to celebrate the birthday of the Church. But should we not commemorate the day by remembering how the Holy Spirit filled the believers, how 3,000 were baptized and how the Church began to march across the Roman Empire and beyond in earnest after the resurrection and ascension of Jesus? Additionally, might the Lord also want us to get ready for deeper life in Him and a harvest of souls in our own local churches?

This little devotional and discussion guide attempts to aid in that preparation for Pentecost. It is designed for married couples, families, friends, small groups or churches to read a daily passage concerning the Holy Spirit, delve into its meaning and then challenge each other with a discussion question or two. Prayer prompts are provided to help participants cultivate open hearts to live out the Spirit's call.

Suggested weekly memory verses are intended to focus the mind on the things of the Spirit. Some churches will choose to have small group studies and sermons to buttress the devotional material.

Enjoy your Holy Spirit journey. If it is Pentecost you are counting towards, it should be your most prepared for, and, therefore, your best Spirit holiday ever. If it is simply personal enrichment another time of the year, may God richly bless you with His purifying, empowering Presence.

Day One

Week One Memory Verse: Matthew 28:19-20 (see pg. 54)

Today's Verse: "Go therefore and make disciples of all nations, baptizing them in the name of the Father and of the Son and of the Holy Spirit, teaching them to observe all that I have commanded you. And behold, I am with you always, to the end of the age." (Matthew 28:18-20)

After the resurrection Jesus tells the disciples what He wants them to do in a passage that has come to be known as The Great Commission. "Go and make disciples," He says, "baptizing them in the name of the Father and of the Son and of the Holy Spirit…" In other words, the name, the authority, the character of what we know today as the Trinity was to be central in the lives of new believers. Baptize them in that name! Now, these disciples of Christ were familiar with the Father, had spent three years with the Son Jesus but had yet to be filled with the Spirit. When the fullness of the Trinity's work in their lives became reality on the day of Pentecost, their lives would be wildly different.

We know many truths about the Trinity, among them these:

1) The love of the Father, Son and Holy Spirit was outgoing…it wasn't containable. Their love was headed out the proverbial door.

2) We have been created and saved by that Trinitarian outgoing love.

3) Others, through the Spirit in us, will experience God as we emulate the outward-bound Trinity. The Spirit-filled person and Church can't/won't be contained!

Questions: If the Trinity is all about outgoing love, what should that mean for our lives? How can we best exhibit outgoing love in our community today? The Trinity wants us to join their team in this saving work - how can we help God share love with our unchurched friends, relatives, associates and neighbors?

Prayer Request: By name, pray for some unchurched friends, relatives, associates and neighbors that they may be touched by the love of the Spirit .

Day Two

Week One Memory Verse: Matthew 28:19-20

Today's Verse: "But the Helper, the Holy Spirit, whom the Father will send in my name, he will teach you all things and bring to your remembrance all that I have said to you." (John 14:26)

In the last week of Jesus' life He tells the disciples that He will not be physically with them much longer, but that the Holy Spirit is coming. And "he will teach you." The Holy Spirit is a teaching Spirit.

A serious educator will tell you that this teaching/learning challenge is about much more than getting a brain-full of important facts. It is about a changed life. Transformation is the point, not jotting answers down for some exam. That is why learning means "changed behavior." Not just head knowledge, but how we actually live our lives. God can change that. The Spirit, if allowed, will change that.

When the central dynamics of our lives are buttressed by the Holy Spirit, then the reaction – the way we actually conduct our lives – will be Christ-like. So let's allow the Spirit to instruct us to the very depths of our souls, and anticipate we will change to be like Him.

But how does that Spirit teach?

- As we study the Bible, asking how we can apply the principles to our life.
- As we pray in such a way that we hear God telling us what we can do with Truth, today.
- As we serve those in need, letting the Spirit remind us that Jesus' greatest teaching moments occurred when He and the disciples were responding to the poor and needy.
- As we faithfully accept the Spirit's moment-by-moment guidance to do the seemingly impossible – forgive, for instance!

Questions: What might the Holy Spirit want to teach me today? An important lesson the Spirit has taught me lately?

Prayer Request: Ask that God might use the Holy Spirit to teach you something truly life-changing.

Day Three

Week One Memory Verse: Matthew 28:19-20

Today's Verse: "But you will receive power when the Holy Spirit has come upon you, and you will be my witnesses in Jerusalem and in all Judea and Samaria, and to the end of the earth." (Acts 1:8)

After the resurrection Jesus instructs His disciples to go to Jerusalem and wait for the Holy Spirit. It is not the first time God had said such a thing to His chosen. In Isaiah 43 God describes a courtroom scene and asks that the gods bring in their witnesses to prove they were right. This is as close to Old Testament humor as it gets for the "gods" have no witnesses, certainly no credible ones!

But then God turns to His chosen people and says "You are my witnesses." Sobering! God's reputation would ride on these people. The problem, of course, is that God's reputation suffered mightily after this passage in Isaiah for they were lousy witnesses. From that point on they lied, cheated, stole, worshipped other gods, abused the poor, lacked justice, and dishonored God.

In Acts, the people would have an advantage over those associated with the account of Isaiah. They were to wait for the Holy Spirit and Jesus promises then they would be His witnesses at home and abroad. God's reputation would thus be on the rise.

Augustine said, "Without the Spirit we can neither love God nor keep His commandments." With the Spirit, we can. We can!

That same Spirit is available to us.

Questions: What is there about the Spirit that made the people in Acts, and people today, good witnesses? What does it mean to be a good witness today?

Prayer Request: The two "you wills" are necessarily wed in today's verse. Review them and pray to receive the Spirit and be a good witness for the Lord.

Day Four

Week One Memory Verse: Matthew 28:19-20

Today's Verse: "And the Holy Spirit descended on him in bodily form like a dove." (Luke 3:22)

There is a story of an Oriental man who came to Christianity. When he first saw the symbol of the Holy Spirit (a descending dove) he said to the missionary who converted him: "Honorable Father very good; Honorable Son very good; but Honorable Bird I don't understand at all!"

All the Gospels tell of Jesus being baptized and, as noted in today's verse, the Holy Spirit came down not just as spirit but in a bodily shape. Because it was like a dove many today think of the spirit as dove-like.

The Celtic Christians had a different idea. They thought of the Spirit as "Ah Geadh-Glas", or the wild goose. A bit strange, perhaps, but the idea had a long tradition in Ireland. Honestly, it is kind of a fun thought, and perhaps with some theological insight. Because in Acts the Holy Spirit can seem a bit wild, untamed, sometimes awkward, noisy and intimidating.

As a boy I used to walk home from school past a yard with pet geese. When they saw me coming, they would point their beaks right at me, flap their wings wildly and come running while honking vociferously. Scared me daily. Now? Well, I have a new appreciation for those geese and what God may have been trying to tell me.

The Spirit comes in Acts and big things happen. Sometimes these things are awkward. And sometimes noisy. And sometimes intimidating. But we are not in control of all of that. The Holy Goose does things in His own way. But I also won't discount the dove. The Holy Dove does some of His best work in a quiet, peaceful, unassuming manner.

Questions: The Holy Spirit as a Goose – any applicable insights you can think of? Why might we prefer to think of the Spirit as Dove, instead?

Prayer Request: Pray to God the Dove – for His quiet, peaceful, movement in my life. Pray to God the Goose – for his loud, big, intimidating movement in our lives.

Day Five

Week One Memory Verse: Matthew 28:19-20

Today's Verse: "But I tell you the truth: It is for your good that I am going away. Unless I go away, the Counselor will not come to you; but if I go, I will send him to you. When he comes, he will convict the world of guilt in regard to sin and righteousness and judgment…" (John 16:7-8)

Prior to Pentecost there was much that was unconverted in the disciples. In Jesus' time with them these are the things that rose to the surface:

- Egoism – they quarreled over who was first.
- Self-righteousness – "Even if all fall away…I never will."
- Resentments – "Lord, do you want us to call fire down from heaven to destroy them?"
- Spiritual impotence – "Why couldn't we drive it out?"
- Criticism – "Why this waste?"
- Bigotry – "We told him to stop because he was not one of us."
- Racism – "Send her away (a Canaanite) for she keeps crying out after us."
- Selfishness – "We have left everything to follow you. What then will there be for us?"
- Fear – "the doors were locked for fear of the Jews"[1]

When Pentecost and the Holy Spirit came, all this changed.

Questions: What are the opposites of all these characteristics (when you discover this, you will have substantially described holy character)? Why did the physical Jesus have to leave before the spiritual Counselor could come? Which of these characteristics is the Spirit talking to you about?

Prayer Request: Pray that the Spirit would convict you of sin, of weakness, of necessary improvement.

Day Six

Week One Memory Verse: Matthew 28:19-20

Today's Verse: "When the day of Pentecost came, they were all together in one place." (Acts 2:1)

There was a time, says E. Stanley Jones, when the Christian Church celebrated Pentecost (sometimes called Whitsunday) more than it did Christmas. Now, Pentecost has largely dropped off the calendar for too many churches.

> Did we find it easier to commemorate his coming into the world than it was for us to go with his message into the world? Did it cost less to give gifts at Christmas than to give ourselves at Pentecost? Christmas is the festival of God with us. Pentecost is the festival of God in us. Is he more with us than in us?[2]

Pentecost is a celebration worth having, for it reminds us of some important things.

> Draw a line through the New Testament and on one side is spiritual fumbling, hesitancy, inadequacy, defeat, and on the other side is certainty, courage, adequacy, victory. That line runs straight through Pentecost.[3]

Questions: We celebrate Christmas and Easter – why don't we do a better job with Pentecost? How could we more wholeheartedly celebrate Pentecost this year as a family and as a church? Why did the fullness of the Spirit on the day of Pentecost make such an incredible difference?

Prayer Request: That God would help us celebrate Pentecost this year with unprecedented passion. That we could have a Pentecostal moment even now – allowing Him to fill us to the brim with His love, purity, and power – with Himself!

Day Seven

Week One Memory Verse: Matthew 28:19-20

Today's Verse: "'As the Father has sent me, I am sending you.' And with that he breathed on them and said, 'Receive the Holy Spirit.'" (John 20:21-22)

After the resurrection John reports that Jesus appeared to His disciples and talked about sending them as He had been sent by the Father. Then He immediately breathed on them. In the Hebrew language breath-wind-spirit are all one word – ruach. Jesus breathing on them might have puzzled the disciples momentarily, but the next four words would have clarified the lesson in their minds: Receive the Holy Spirit.

Whatever happened with that graphic portrayal it was less than what would happen with the Spirit at Pentecost. Almost assuredly, it was preparatory, but what powerful preparation! The actual breath of the resurrected Lord and those precious four words in rapid succession may well have sent two great Old Testament events through their minds in reflection – Genesis 1, when God breathed into Adam the breath of life; the Ezekiel 37 when God's ruach animated dry bones.

Jesus made it clear what their new life would be like: I am sending you. He also said during these days: Go and make disciples of all nations (Mt. 28:19-20). On the day of His ascension He tells them to be his witnesses to the ends of the earth (Acts 1:8). Their lives were no longer stay-at-home affairs. They were now "sent" people.

You and I need to be open to going to other nations. But whether we ever feel God's call on our lives for that we are nonetheless sent people. We are redesigned in the Spirit to get out of our homes and churches and go to where lost, lonely, hurting people without Christ live. That is our destiny as "breathed on" men and women.

Questions: The Spirit and "sending" are a package deal. Are we comfortable with that?

Prayer Request: Pray that we feel the breath of Jesus on our lives and will be willing to go where He wants us to go.

Day Eight

Week Two Memory Verse: 2 Corinthians 3:17 (see pg. 54)

Today's Verse: "Then the Spirit of the Lord came upon Gideon, and he blew a trumpet, summoning the Abiezrites to follow him." (Judges 6:34)

I was zipping along in my NIV Study Bible one morning, anxious to get to a favorite chapter – when Gideon defeats the Midianites. Before that, however, came a line from the previous chapter: The Spirit...came upon. My study Bible noted: this means literally (in the Hebrew) the "Spirit...clothed himself with." Further, "This vivid figure, used only three times (in the Bible) emphasizes that the Spirit of the Lord empowered the human agent and acted through him."

Sure enough, the word for "came" there is lavash, which means to put on clothes/to wear. What an honor! God chooses to wear Gideon. The argument could be made that the usage of that word is so rare in the Scripture that this only happens in special circumstances when God really wants something big done. Perhaps. But equally as valid a thought is this - today, in the circumstances where God places us, there are many special circumstances; God really wants some important things done in our spheres of experience and influence. If that is the case, most of the time the decision will be ours – God is ready to wear us, to clothe Himself with us, if we are willing.

If God wearing us is rare, then I suppose it could also be said that this is because too many of us prefer not to be worn by God and have voted in favor of our filthy rags instead.

Many times I have been in a difficult situation wondering what to do, how to behave, what to say right before somebody walks up and performs marvelously with the Spirit of Christ all over their actions in those moments. I sometimes wonder if I can't I hear the Lord saying: I wanted to use you that way but you wouldn't let me clothe myself with you.

Questions: Think of your most difficult moment today – what might have happened if the Spirit were wearing you? Why wouldn't someone want to be worn by God?

Prayer Request: As passionately as you can (but only if you really want it!) "Clothe yourself with me, Spirit of God."

Day Nine

Week Two Memory Verse: 2 Corinthians 3:17

Today's Verse: "Anyone who speaks a word against the Son of Man will be forgiven, but anyone who speaks against the Holy Spirit will not be forgiven, either in this age or in the age to come." (Matthew 12:32)

Many people have wondered, "Have I committed that horrific, unforgiveable sin?"

Since it is best to look at biblical texts in their context, let's start there. In Matthew, Jesus has just healed a demon-possessed man who was blind and mute. The Pharisees then said, "It is only by Beelzebub, the prince of demons, that this fellow drives out demons."

In the Old Testament, deliberate blasphemy against God could not be atoned for under Old Testament law and was punishable by death. (Leviticus 24:10-23).[4] It was a serious matter.

Here is what is happening, apparently, in the Gospels. The Pharisees see the Holy Spirit at work through Jesus. But they have another conception of Messiah than Jesus is representing and, beyond that, Jesus continually embarrasses them in debate. They can't stand it! So, instead of acknowledging the obvious gracious work of God through Jesus, they declare accusatory war on Him. He is of the devil! In cahoots with the Beelzebub - "prince of demons!" They know better.

There is a serious warning here. If you get to the point in your life where you are saying or doing things continually against God's will – whom you have encountered – that you know simply aren't true or right, you may well have come to the place where your heart is so hardened that you wouldn't consider repenting. God is capable of hardening hearts; but, sometimes, our own words and actions can harden our hearts to the place of "no return." What a terrible kind of "hard" this is.

Questions: How can the pronouncements of your mouth impact your heart? Where does God need to soften your hard heart?

Prayer Request: Pray that God tenderizes your heart and the hearts of those who don't yet know Him.

Day Ten

Week Two Memory Verse: 2 Corinthians 3:17

Today's Verse: "At once the Spirit sent him out into the desert, and he was in the desert forty days, being tempted by Satan." (Mark 1:12-13)

The Spirit sent Jesus to be tempted - a most curious phrase of Scripture. Why would the Spirit do such a thing to Jesus and, if He did it to Jesus, might He do it to us? Probably, truth be known.

The extended temptation narratives of Matthew and Luke have Jesus out in a Judean desert battling with Satan. The devil comes at Jesus and tempts Him to take an easier path:

- Make bread out of stones to assuage the hunger.

- Worship the devil and receive the kingdoms of the world.

- Throw Himself off the temple and immediately receive the comfort and care of angels.

All of these were incisive temptations because of context. Out in the desert life is hard, unforgiving, lonely; basically, a depriving experience that renders us vulnerable. And yet, Jesus was undeterred. His emergence from the desert precipitated a flurry of spiritual activity. And that is the point. Jesus, full of the Holy Spirit, is led by that same Spirit to a hard, trying, unforgiving, lonely place. He shows us that when we make it out of the desert places of life with integrity intact true holiness will start to make its momentous march across the globe.

Count on it – desert times are coming. And the Spirit might just lead us there. If we come out of that desert like Jesus did, our spiritual influence may well will be on the move with renewed vigor.

Question: What desert experiences have we had that God has used? What scares us about the desert?

Prayer Request: Pray that the Spirit leads us into any experience, desert or otherwise, that expands our influence for Him.

Day Eleven

Week Two Memory Verse: 2 Corinthians 3:17

Today's Verse: "The Holy Spirit will come upon you, and the power of the Most High will overshadow you. So the holy one to be born will be called the Son of God." (Luke 1:35)

There is, says Clarence Jordan, a very close similarity between the two biographies of Jesus, and the Church, at the point of the birth narratives.

- In the first volume of Luke, Mary is his mother. God implants Jesus in her womb. A Son of God came forth to change the world.

- In the second volume of Luke (which is Acts), the Church takes the place of Mary and God implants his Holy Spirit in the womb of the Church to bring forth a new kind of son and daughter of God to change the world.

- As Jesus preached, taught and healed so the sons and daughters of God are to do the same today. As Jesus made disciples, so too are the children of the second birth narrative of Luke.[5]

This is the privilege of the Church - to become the womb of God through which He can bring his children into this world. There are ways to prevent pregnancies, of course, but the Church must be pro-child and pro-life at the point of bringing many children to life by His grace. The Holy Spirit is ready and, undoubtedly remembers, that the first command of God in Genesis was "Be fruitful and multiply!"

Questions: What are examples of why the Church might not want more children? What prevents us from having them?

Prayer Request: Pray that we would want "babies" – new Christians – as much as the Holy Spirit wants them.

Day Twelve

Week Two Memory Verse: 2 Corinthians 3:17

Today's Verse: "Ananias, how is it that Satan has so filled your heart that you have lied to the Holy Spirit..." (Acts 5:3)

If you take up the book of Acts and start reading you will be able to note, as John Stott has, that the chief actor of the first couple of chapters is the Holy Spirit. But, says Stott, the chief actor "in Acts 3-6 almost seems to be Satan. True, he is identified only once by name, but his activity may be discerned throughout...The devil cannot endure the exaltation of Jesus Christ."[6]

John Calvin on the same matter:

> As soon as the truth of the Gospel comes to light, Satan sets himself in opposition to it by every means in his power, and uses every endeavour to crush it in its earliest beginnings.[7]

Some time ago I picked up the Journal of Francis Asbury, the early Methodist preacher sent by John Wesley to spark Methodism in the colonies. There was no doubt in his mind that Satan was hard at work against his ministry. Over and over again you read things like this:

> I believe Satan has been hard at work, and has painted every possible danger he can to my imagination. (May 29, 1781)

> My soul is given up to God; but I have felt Satan near. Lord, help, or I perish! (November 5, 1787)

> ...it is hard to civilize, methodize, and spiritualize: sin, Satan, flesh, and hell are against us. (March 18, 1792)

When the narrative of the Spirit begins in earnest, so does the narrative of spiritual warfare. Let us not be surprised by this. Certainly, God isn't.

Questions: Should we be dismayed that Satan is at work? What does spiritual warfare mean for us?

Prayer Request: Pray God would make us fit for the war. Pray for the individual placement of the armor of God (Eph. 6:11-14)

Day Thirteen

Week Two Memory Verse: 2 Corinthians 3:17

Today's Verse: "And they were all filled with the Holy Spirit and spoke the word of God boldly." (Acts 4:31)

Have we cheapened the term revival? A dictionary definition suggests that revival means "a period in which something becomes popular again after a long period of time." Some churches have revival services annually to, presumably, make vibrant Christianity popular again. But, if the official definition rings true, what exactly is it that was once popular and worth renewing?

Could Acts 4:23-35 point the way? The believers were "filled with the Holy Spirit"; perhaps we could get some guidance as to what that early church looked like when this happened. Read the passage and see if your list corresponds to this one:

- They were emboldened:
    - To pray together
    - Talk about Scripture
    - Pray for courage and miraculous signs and wonders

- Their meeting place was shaken
- They spoke the Word of God boldly
- There was unity of hearts and minds
- There was economic liberality, sharing
- There was testifying power
- Grace was on them all

It may well be worth asking if this is what happens as a result of the special services we call "revivals." It certainly seems to be a beautiful picture of corporate holiness.

Questions: Of these characteristics, what items are most like our church? Least like it? What might it mean that "grace was on them all"?

Prayer Request: Pray that we might be revived like this. Ask that God would use you to help revive your church by His Spirit and His grace.

Day Fourteen

Week Two Memory Verse: 2 Corinthians 3:17

Today's Verse: "All over the world this gospel is bearing fruit and growing just as it has been doing among you since the day you heard it and understood God's grace in all its truth." (Col. 1:6)

In 2007 Newsweek magazine asked author and radio personality Garrison Keillor what he considered to be the five most important books. Keillor's personal commitment to Christianity is not known although judging by his humor he obviously has a deep respect for the faith. Even so, some were probably a bit startled to find Acts at the top of his ranking of important volumes. Keillor offered this summation: "The flames lit on their little heads and bravely and dangerously went they onward."[8]

Filled with the Holy Spirit, Paul could brag about these scattered people in his letters just a few decades after Pentecost:

- "First, I thank my God through Jesus Christ for all of you, because your faith is being reported all over the world." (Rom. 1:8)

- "All over the world this gospel is bearing fruit and growing... (Col. 1:6)

Not long after that Justin Martyr (100?-165?) would say this (and it was by no means a unique testimony):

- "There is not a single race of human beings, barbarians, Greeks, or whatever name you please to call them, nomads or vagrants or herdsmen living in tents, where prayers in the name of Jesus the crucified are not offered up. Through all the members of the body is the soul spread; so are Christians throughout the cities of the world."

When the Holy Spirit alights, Christians go forward bravely, dangerously and with great effectiveness.

Questions: What inhibits Holy Spirit effectiveness in and through us?

Prayer Request: Pray for Holy Spirit effectiveness in evangelism.

Day Fifteen

Week Three Memory Verse: John 14:15-17 (see pg. 54)

Today's Verse: "Love the Lord your God with all your heart and with all your soul and with all your mind." (Matthew 22:37)

The typical evangelistic plea to those who have yet to receive the Lord is "Accept Jesus as your personal Savior...let Him come and sit on the throne of your life" or words to that effect. So – what about the Holy Spirit? Is it just Jesus who enters into a person receiving Christ, or does, say, the Spirit come with Him?

When Jesus comes, so does the Spirit. So, the Spirit resides in all believers. But the Spirit needs to be let loose into every nook and cranny of your life.

James Emery White demonstrates it in this way. Imagine two glasses of water and two packets of Alka-Seltzer. Drop a packet of Alka-Seltzer with the wrapper on, into a glass. Then plop an unsealed packet into the second glass, and watch it fill with fizz.

Says White, "Both glasses have the Alka-Seltzer, just as all Christians have the Holy Spirit. But notice how you can have the Holy Spirit and not his filling."[9]

We need to let the Spirit loose in our lives. He wants to be allowed into every bit of our lives – attitudes, relationships, finances, sexuality, ambitions. The Spirit is willing. Are we?

Questions: What prevents us from letting the Spirit loose in the totality of our lives? If there is one area that you suspect the Spirit would love to invade in your heart, what would that be?

Prayer Request: Pray that God would give you the grace to decide for the unleashing of the Spirit into ALL of your life.

Day Sixteen

Week Three Memory Verse: John 14:15-17

Today's Verse: "In the beginning God created the heavens and the earth. Now the earth was formless and empty, darkness was over the face of the deep, and the Spirit of God was hovering over the waters." (Genesis 1:1-2)

The Hebrew word for "spirit" is ruach which, as it has been said, can mean breath, wind or spirit. So, imagine the breath of God hovering above an abyss, getting ready to perform creatively. Below that Spirit is:

- Formlessness
- Emptiness
- Darkness

But the Breath, the Wind, the Spirit of God is poised to change all that. The Egyptian view of origins is helpful, actually, at this point. According to their understanding, the concept of nonexistence (much like formlessness, emptiness and darkness) means "that which has not yet been differentiated and assigned function. No boundaries or definition have been established."[10]

When the Spirit does His work in the Church there comes, from this initial state,

- Godly form,
- Holy fullness and
- the Light of His glory.

Enlivened by the Spirit of God, there comes a people made with and for a holy difference, with assigned roles in the Kingdom, who work within righteous boundaries and with gracious definition.

Questions: Imagine the Spirit hovering over your family or group or church right now. What does He want to do next? What new thing might He want to create?

Prayer Request: Pray that we might allow the Spirit of God to do whatever He wants. Most of all, that He would bring to us godly form, holy fullness and His light to make a holy difference through the roles He assigns us.

Day Seventeen

Week Three Memory Verse: John 14:15-17

Today's Verse: "In the church at Antioch…they were worshiping the Lord and fasting, the Holy Spirit said, 'Set apart for me Barnabas and Saul for the work to which I have called them.' So after they had fasted and prayed, they placed their hands on them and sent them off." (Acts 13:1-3)

The Great Commission had already begun in Acts when the church at Antioch was found worshipping, praying and fasting. But it continued in earnest in Acts 13 with the launching of Saul/Paul's great missionary work. This was nearly a decade after Saul's conversion, and he must have been chomping at the bit to get moving in the direction Jesus had initially told him he would go.

But the great missionary movement of arguably the greatest missionary ever began with adoration and the spiritual disciplines. That worship is essential won't boggle the imagination of most believers. That praying had to take place before this epochal moment will not surprise. But what of the fasting?

In our verses for today worshipping is mentioned once. Praying also gets a single mention. But fasting – twice. This discipline of the faith that is rarely practiced today with any kind of regularity among the vast majority of Christians was apparently central to the Church at this time and made them missionally robust in the hands of the Holy Spirit.

The Didache, an early Church manual, suggested that the Church fast regularly on Wednesdays and Fridays. While many modern Christians might be dubious, the early Church thought there was power in regular self-denial of food when coupled with worship and praying. At Antioch, the Holy Spirit spoke through their discipline and sent two of them to the nations with the Gospel.

Questions: What is there about self-denial via fasting that enables the Spirit to speak to and act through us?

Prayer Request: Pray for a fresh awareness of fasting and self-denial that the Spirit might move mightily and missionally.

Day Eighteen

Week Three Memory Verse: John 14:15-17

Today's Verse: "Create in me a pure heart, O God, and renew a steadfast spirit within me. Do not cast me from your presence or take your Holy Spirit from me. Restore to me the joy of your salvation and grant me a willing spirit, to sustain me." (Psalm 51:10-12)

Notice that today's verse has two small "s" spirits and one capital "S" Spirit. David wants a steadfast spirit and a willing spirit. To get these he knows the Holy Spirit will be necessary.

But David is worried. He has sinned mightily as the king who was supposed to be setting a holy example for his nation. David sees another man's wife and through several egregious actions commits

- Adultery
- False witness
- Murder
- And produces a baby that immediately dies because of his transgressions...

In the midst of this famous prayer of David (Ps. 51) he says, "Do not cast me from your presence or take your Holy Spirit from me." David, as a younger man, had seen, first-hand, what happens when the Spirit leaves a man. Basically, he goes crazy.

> [14] Now the Spirit of the LORD had departed from Saul, and an evil spirit from the LORD tormented him. (1 Samuel 16:14)

So, of all things necessary, "Take not thy Holy Spirit from me." David wants the presence of God, His Spirit, and his sanity.

Questions: If the Holy Spirit left you, what difference would it make?

Prayer Request: Pray for God's presence and His Spirit in your life. Pray that He will give you the desire for this above all things.

Day Nineteen

Week Three Memory Verse: John 14:15-17

Today's Verse: "May God himself, the God of peace, sanctify you through and through. May your whole spirit, soul and body be kept blameless at the coming of our Lord Jesus Christ." (1 Thess. 5:23)

Telling the Spirit of God to take over your life is no small thing. The step from born-again Christian to Spirit-filled believer is huge. This is what John Wesley said about what was at stake:

"Well may a man ask his own heart, whether it is able to admit the Spirit of God...

- For where that divine Guest enters, the laws of another world must be observed.

- The body must be given up to martyrdom, or spent in the Christian warfare, as unconcernedly as if the soul were already provided of its house from heaven;

- the goods of this world must be parted with as freely, as if the last fire were to seize them to-morrow;

- our neighbor must be loved as heartily as if he were washed from all his sins, and demonstrated to be a child of God by the resurrection from the dead.

- The fruits of this Spirit must not be mere moral virtues, calculated for the comfort and decency of the present life; but holy dispositions, suitable to the instincts of a superior life already begun...[11]

Wesley mentions "the superior life." The fruit of the Spirit is, basically, Christ-likeness. Being like Jesus is what life in the Spirit is all about.

Questions: Of the above statements of Wesley which are the most challenging?

Prayer Request: Pray for the expansion of the Spirit-life in you, your family, and your church.

Day Twenty

Week Three Memory Verse: John 14:15-17

Today's Verse: "Jesus looked at them and said, 'With man this is impossible, but with God all things are possible.'" (Matthew 19:26)

Dwight L. Moody was a shoe salesman who was beginning to wonder if God might have some ministry direction for him. Early one morning he gathered with a number of friends in a field for a season of prayer. His friend Henry Varley, a British revivalist who had befriended the young American, said during that gathering, "The world has yet to see what God can do with and for and through and in a man who is fully and wholly consecrated to Him." Those words shook Moody.

He later went to a meeting where Charles Spurgeon was preaching. In that meeting Moody recalled the words spoken by his friend, "The world has yet to see ... with and for and through and in ... a man!" Moody thought "Varley meant any man! Varley didn't say he had to be educated, or brilliant, or anything else. Just a man!" Well, by the Holy Spirit in him, he'd be one of those men! He recognized that, after all, it was not Spurgeon moving the souls of people; it was God. If God could use Spurgeon, why should He not use the rest of us, and why should we not all just lay ourselves at the Master's feet and say to Him, "Send me! Use me!"?[12]

The key words for us are these: fully, wholly consecrated. That is our part. Sanctifying and making that consecration of ourselves holy? That is God's part.

He is ready, if we are.

Questions: What keeps people from fully, wholly consecrating themselves before God?

Prayer Request: Pray that you might be wholly, fully consecrated to God.

Day Twenty-One

Week Three Memory Verse: John 14:15-17

Today's Verse: "Be perfect, therefore, as your heavenly Father is perfect." (Matthew 5:48)

So...let's get our orthodoxy, our doctrine straight. That will make us all good Christians, right?

John Wesley didn't think so.

> "...neither does religion consist in Orthodoxy, or right opinions; which, although they are not properly outward things, are not in the heart, but the understanding.
>
> A man may be orthodox in every point; he may not only espouse right opinions, but zealously defend them against all opposers; he may think justly concerning the incarnation of our Lord, concerning the ever-blessed Trinity, and every other doctrine contained in the oracles of God; he may assent to all the three creeds, -- that called the Apostles', the Nicene, and the Athanasian; and yet it is possible he may have no religion at all, no more than a Jew, Turk, or pagan.
>
> He may be almost as orthodox -- as the devil, (though, indeed, not altogether; for every man errs in something; whereas we can't well conceive him to hold any erroneous opinion,) and may, all the while be as great a stranger as he to the religion of the heart.
>
> This alone is religion, truly so called: This alone is in the sight of God of great price. The Apostle sums it all up in three particulars, "righteousness, and peace, and joy in the Holy Ghost." (Romans 14:7)[13]

"In the Holy Ghost" was the key, not orthodoxy. We want both – but we want the Holy Spirit the most. It leads to all other good things.

Questions: What happens if we take more pleasure in right doctrine over an on-going love relationship with God?

Request: Pray for a loving relationship with God for all your family and church AND that the Spirit will help you grasp correct belief.

Day Twenty-Two

Week Four Memory Verse: Ezekiel 36:26-27 (see pg. 54)

Today's Verse: "Then Peter said, 'Silver or gold I do not have, but what I do have I give you. In the name of Jesus Christ of Nazareth, walk.'" (Acts 3:6)

What happens after the Holy Spirit comes In Acts 2 is instructive. The primary founder of the Nazarenes was Phineas Bresee and this is what he noticed in the subsequent chapters of Acts.

> The first miracle after the baptism of the Holy Ghost was wrought upon a beggar. It means that the first service of a Holy Ghost-baptized church is to the poor; that its ministry is to those who are lowest down; that its gifts are for those who need them the most. As the Spirit was upon Jesus to preach the gospel to the poor, so His Spirit is upon His servants for the same purpose.

Other quotes of Bresee's reflected this insight. His dream for the new denomination went along these lines:

- "We can get along without rich people, but not without preaching the gospel to the poor."

- "We want pastors who will go out and find the poor that nobody else cares for."

- "The evidence of the presence of Jesus in our midst is that we bear the gospel, primarily, to the poor. This must be genuine; it is more than sentiment; it cannot be simulated nor successfully imitated."

- "Let the Church of the Nazarene be true to its commission; not great and elegant buildings; but to feed the hungry and clothe the naked, and wipe away the tears of sorrowing, and gather jewels for His diadem."

Questions: Until the Holy Spirit fills us we are reluctant to reach out to the poor – why?

Prayer Request: Pray we would have the same heart and hands for the poor in our community that God has.

Day Twenty-Three

Week Four Memory Verse: Ezekiel 36:26-27

Today's Verse: (They have) "a form of godliness but denying its power." (2 Tim. 3:5)

General William Booth of the Salvation Army said that "The chief danger that confronts the coming century will be...

- religion without the Holy Ghost,
- Christianity without Christ,
- forgiveness without repentance,
- salvation without regeneration,
- politics without God,
- heaven without hell."[14]

The General had that right. And the next century, as well as the current one, deals with these "dangers." Let's take a closer look at that first one...what does "religion without the Holy Ghost" look like?

- Going through the motions of church, without life transformation.
- A movement hopelessly and selfishly turned inward.
- A disregard for the poor, the disenfranchised, the lost, the lonely.
- Holiness without holy love.
- A lack of lavish giving.
- Popular culture inspires, the breath of God is not felt.
- Sexual immorality, impurity and debauchery; idolatry and witchcraft; hatred, discord, jealousy, fits of rage, selfish ambition, dissensions, factions and envy; drunkenness, orgies, and the like. (Gal. 5:19-21)

Perhaps we could go on? This is the gist of life without the Spirit. The Spirit is given that we might have freedom from such a life. Booth mentioned six items; it could be easily argued that the latter five come from the first.

Questions: Can you note biblical illustrations for each of Booth's warnings? Which are you most vulnerable to?

Prayer Request: Pray the Spirit delivers us from the consequences of life without Him.

Day Twenty-Four

Week Four Memory Verse: Ezekiel 36:26-27

Today's Verse: "I am the Lord your God; consecrate yourselves and be holy, because I am holy." (Leviticus 11:44)

The late Dr. A. W. Tozer, author and pastor, said,

> If the Holy Spirit was withdrawn from the church today, 95 percent of what we do would go on and no one would know the difference. If the Holy Spirit had been withdrawn from the New Testament church, 95 percent of what they did would stop, and everybody would know the difference.

That invites some interesting analysis – ask, "How much of what this family/church/group/friendship does is dependent on the Holy Spirit?" And, "What would be different with us if the Holy Spirit had no control over what we thought/felt/did?"

The Hebrew word for "profane" is khalal meaning "common." The opposite of common/profane is "holy"/qadosh and it means, among other things, "different." When the Qadosh Spirit comes into our lives we should be different as He is different. E. Stanley Jones said that "If God is a Christlike God, then it follows that the Spirit is a Christlike Spirit. The same content of character will be in both. Then if the Spirit lives within us, He will not make us other than Christlike."[15]

To be Christlike is to be uncommon. If the Church is not Christlike, because it lacks the Christlike Spirit, then we should not be surprised that our surrounding unchurched community – which is watching – will know the difference. And yet, occasionally, there arises a Christlike Church which, because of that Christlike Spirit within exhibits vibrancy, love, outgoing purpose and, basically, a revival of discipleship.

Questions: Where do you see the Hoy Spirit at work in your church? How do you know?

Prayer Request: Pray that the Christlike Spirit will continue to make you/your group/your church, Christlike.

Day Twenty-Five

Week Four Memory Verse: Ezekiel 36:26-27

Today's Verse: "Now an angel of the Lord said to Philip, 'Go south to the road--the desert road--that goes down from Jerusalem to Gaza.' So he started out, and on his way he met an Ethiopian eunuch, an important official in charge of all the treasury of Candace, queen of the Ethiopians. This man had gone to Jerusalem to worship, and on his way home was sitting in his chariot reading the book of Isaiah the prophet. The Spirit told Philip, 'Go to that chariot and stay near it.' Then Philip ran up to the chariot…" (Acts 8:26-30)

If you are someone who likes to share their faith, the story of Philip and the Ethiopian eunuch will undoubtedly be a favorite. Philip, as it might be remembered, was chosen in Acts 6 to be a deacon because he was "full of the Spirit and wisdom." Not long after that we find him on a desert road and God needs an evangelist.

First, God used an angel: "Go south…" And, says Luke, "he started out." Just as simple as that. Directive received – immediate obedience. The expected response of someone "full of the Spirit and wisdom." Then, "The Spirit told Philip, 'Go to that chariot…" and, it is recorded, "Philip ran up to the chariot…"

The ancient rabbis taught that when Abraham heard God instruct him to take his son Isaac and sacrifice him as a burnt offering, his response was most impressive: "Early the next morning Abraham got up…" For these rabbis, the Hebrew phrase for "Early the next morning" were some of the most precious words in all the Torah. No waiting. No sleeping in. No hesitancy. Just go.

When we "start out," "run up" and "get up early" to obey, God blesses. But that blessing is contingent upon the Spirit in us. We don't even have the capacity to hear and start-run-get up without Him.

Questions: What is the Spirit telling you to go and do NOW?

Prayer Request: Pray that we might hear clearly from God and obey immediately.

Day Twenty-Six

Week Four Memory Verse: Ezekiel 36:26-27

Today's Verse: "'Come, follow me,' Jesus said, 'and I will make you fishers of men.'" (Matthew 4:19)

The 1974 International Congress on World Evangelization was one of the most consequential Christian gatherings in the last century. It grew into The Lausanne Movement that even today seeks to mobilize evangelical leaders to strategize for world evangelization. Delegates to this gathering drafted a statement on evangelism that has been formative to many who think deeply on this matter. One of the paragraphs out of their "Lausanne Covenant" was about the Holy Spirit. It stated:

> We believe in the power of the Holy Spirit....the Holy Spirit is a missionary spirit; thus evangelism should arise spontaneously from a Spirit-filled church. A church that is not a missionary church is contradicting itself and quenching the Spirit. Worldwide evangelization will become a realistic possibility only when the Spirit renews the Church in truth and wisdom, faith, holiness, love and power. We therefore call upon all Christians to pray for such a visitation of the sovereign Spirit of God that all his fruit may appear in all his people and that all his gifts may enrich the body of Christ. Only then will the whole church become a fit instrument in his hands, that the whole earth may hear his voice.

Over the next few days we will cover some of the aspects of this paragraph. First, "the Holy Spirit is a missionary Spirit...a church that is not a missionary church is contradicting itself and quenching the Spirit."

Jesus challenged His disciples to "Follow Me." If they didn't, they weren't going to be with Jesus - they couldn't be taught by Him, used of Him, related to Him. For those men to be with Jesus they had to get up from what they were doing and physically follow Him. He was a missionary Savior. And the Spirit is the same. That Spirit is headed out the door. We'd better go with Him.

Questions: If the Spirit heads out of our church weekly, where is He going in our community?

Prayer Request: Pray that you would follow the Spirit to evangelistic and compassionate ministry.

Day Twenty-Seven

Week Four Memory Verse: Ezekiel 36:26-27

Today's Verse: "Do not put out the Spirit's fire." (1 Thess. 5:19)

We continue our study inspired by The Lausanne Covenant: "A church that is not a missionary church is contradicting itself and quenching the Spirit."

I used to give my students a picture of a funnel and instruct them to plot the organization of their church within that diagram, the top of the funnel being the entry point and involving the greatest number of people. The narrowing of the funnel indicated increased commitment levels and fewer participants and, eventually, people leaving the church in ministry to impact culture. But one student's funnel caught my attention. I couldn't quite make out what was at the bottom of Karl's diagram. Instead of arrows heading out of the bottom there was a cork. "Everything is bottled up in my church," he said. "All ministry is kept there to serve the members."

The Church is meant to be poured out into the community and the world. If this doesn't happen, it is not fulfilling its God-given purpose.

The Spirit, like the Son, says "Follow me." If we refuse, then we put out the Spirit's fire. It is not that He isn't alive. It's just that He won't be alive in us anymore. The Spirit is headed out in ministry to the prison, the AIDS hospice, the crisis pregnancy center, the literacy center and, frankly, to all manners of mission fields both domestic and international. If you want the Spirit to be alive in you, you need to go with Him.

Most churches don't. That's why most churches couldn't be mistaken for Spirit-filled ministries. Same goes for small groups, families and individuals. But in step with the Spirit, there is power. And life transformation. And a fleshing out of the Great Commission.

Questions: Is there something daunting about where the Spirit might lead? Is there something even more alarming about refusing to go where He is going?

Prayer Request: Pray we would follow the Spirit to the hard and dark places of our community.

Day Twenty-Eight

Week Four Memory Verse: Ezekiel 36:26-27

Today's Verse: "Do not put out the Spirit's fire." (1 Thess. 5:19)

We continue our study from yesterday. The Lausanne Covenant states, "Worldwide evangelization will become a realistic possibility only when the Spirit renews the Church in truth and wisdom, faith, holiness, love and power."

Now, that is quite a list. The Spirit wants to renew us at the points of...

- Truth – "If you look for truth," says C.S. Lewis, "you may find comfort in the end; if you look for comfort you will not get either comfort or truth only soft soap and wishful thinking to begin, and in the end, despair." Holy Spirit people have a passion for truth.

- Wisdom – Luther said that we admit freely that God is more powerful than we are, but not wiser. We may say he is wiser, "but when it comes to a showdown, we do not want to act on what we say." Holy Spirit people abide moment-by-moment in the belief that God is wiser—which makes us wise.

- Faith – A former professor, Robert Traina, said, "You do what you believe, and you believe what you do." Holy Spirit people not only intellectually affirm beliefs but act on them.

- Holiness – In the children's catechism our family uses, we recite John Wesley's unsurpassed four-pronged definition of holiness: "the love of God and neighbor, the image of God stamped on the heart, the life of God in the soul of man and the mind that was in Christ, enabling us to walk as Jesus also walked." Holy Spirit people reflect this kind of holiness.

- Love – Francois Fenelon said, "God's love is full of consideration, patience, and tenderness. It leads people out of their weakness and sin one step at a time." Holy Spirit people love the way God loves.

- Power – "You shall receive power when the Holy Spirit comes on you..." said Jesus. God is omnipotent. Holy Spirit people tap into that Strength.

Questions: Which of these are most prevalent in your life/our church? Least? Why?

Prayer Request: Pray for Spirit help with your weaknesses on this list.

Day Twenty-Nine

Week Five Memory Verse: Luke 4:18-19 (see pg. 54)

Today's Verse: "But the fruit of the Spirit is love, joy, peace, patience, kindness, goodness, faithfulness, gentleness and self-control." (Galatians 5:22)

The Lausanne Covenant says that we need a "visitation of the sovereign Spirit of God that all his fruit may appear in all his people…"

All His fruit in all His people. A review of Paul's list of fruit (above) shows the character of Christ. Each word is a lifelong study. And the list rightly begins with "the greatest of these" – love. From the love of God and neighbor flows all else. Notice that in Galatians these fruit are contrasted with the "acts" of the sinful nature. These "acts" lead us in several, debilitating directions. "Fruit" is unified, comprehensive, whole.

Does the ripened fruit of the Spirit come all at once in a person's life? Deuteronomy says that the Lord would make His people prosperous in every work of their hands, "in the fruit of thy body, and in the fruit of thy cattle, and in the fruit of thy land, for good" (Dt. 30:9/KJV) At Pentecost, the Spirit came and life changed dramatically, right then! Can we expect that instantaneous miracle with every move of the Spirit in our lives?

Probably not with fruit. When the Spirit saves, the fruit begins to grow. When we give the Spirit full control and become completely His, the growth curve rises dramatically. But even then, time is necessary.

Paul says in this passage, "Since we live by the Spirit, let us keep in step with the Spirit." Keeping in step is the gist of the Spirit-filled life. "We are yoked to One who is trained," says Richard Foster. "Our only task is to keep in step with him. He chooses the direction and leads the way. As we walk step by step with him, we soon discover that we have lost the crushing burden of needing to take care of ourselves and get our own way…We come into the joyful, simple life…"[16]

Questions: Of the fruit, which is the Spirit working to improve in you?

Prayer Request: Pray we might be fruitful – individually, group, family, church. Pray where we need especial grace.

Day Thirty

Week Five Memory Verse: Luke 4:18-19

Today's Verse: "All (the gifts) are the work of one and the same Spirit, and he gives them to each one, just as he determines." (1 Corinthians 12:11)

The Lausanne Covenant, concerning the Holy Spirit, finally suggests that we need a visitation from the "Spirit of God that...all his gifts may enrich the body of Christ. Only then will the whole church become a fit instrument in his hands, that the whole earth may hear his voice."

The gifts, says Paul's first epistle to the Corinthians, are given to people in the Church "for the common good." (12:7) We are given gifts not for ourselves, but for others. Additional lessons from 1 Corinthians 12-13:

- God decides who gets what gift.

- All the gifts are different, all are useful, and no one is inferior because they don't have a certain gift.

- God arranges the gifts in the Church like He arranges the parts of a human body to work together. If one part suffers, the whole body suffers. If one part is honored, the whole body is honored.

- Gifts without love are worthless.

In my profession, I have seen many a great teacher elevated to a position of administration. Teaching and administration are, it seems, two different gifts. And frequently a great teacher, gifted by God to instruct, becomes a poor to mediocre administrator, because he is operating outside his spiritual gifting.

It helps to know your gift and how you can maximize that gift for the purpose of winning and making disciples. To do so will keep you fulfilled and, when enough others in the Body do the same, the Church grows.

Questions: Read Romans 12:6-8 and ask: what is my spiritual gift (or spiritual gift mix)? How about the person next to you?

Prayer Request: Pray God would use His gifts mightily for the common good – the good of the Church and of the unevangelized.

Day Thirty-One

Week Five Memory Verse: Luke 4:18-19

Today's Verse: "But when he, the Spirit of truth comes...He will not speak on his own; he will speak only what hears, and he will tell you what is yet to come." (John 16:13)

I once asked a prominent biblical scholar once why there weren't more good books in our tradition written about the Holy Spirit. He said, "It is because the Holy Spirit doesn't try to draw attention to Himself."

Don Strobe has a sermon titled "The Shy Member of the Trinity." There he says that...

> He never speaks on His own behalf. The Holy Spirit, in other words, does not focus on the Holy Spirit. The Holy Spirit focuses on Christ. That is why we have such foggy perceptions of the Holy Spirit...There is a sense in which the Holy Spirit must always remain in hiding, must always be beyond our human understanding, must always be the mysterious hidden power through whom we touch the deepest recesses of our faith. The ...Holy Spirit never draws attention to Himself, but always points to Jesus Christ. "He will glorify me," said the Lord, "because he will take what is mine and declare it to you."[17]

The "Law of Servanthood" is at work here. The Spirit wants to place the attention on the Son, not Himself. He speaks what He hears from Jesus. He shines the light on Jesus. He helps us become Christlike. And yet, He is no less God than the Father or the Son.

> So the Father is God, the Son is God, and the Holy Spirit is God;
> And yet they are not three Gods, but one God.
> So likewise the Father is Lord, the Son Lord, and the Holy Spirit Lord;
> And yet they are not three Lords but one Lord...
> But the whole three persons are coeternal, and coequal.[18]

Questions: The Spirit doesn't draw attention to Himself but to Christ – why is this important? What happens if too much attention goes to the Spirit? What lessons about service can we learn from the Spirit?

Prayer Request: Pray that the Spirit helps us "fix our eyes on Jesus."

Day Thirty-Two

Week Five Memory Verse: Luke 4:18-19

Today's Verse: "Offer your bodies as living sacrifices, holy and pleasing to God – this is your spiritual act of worship." (Romans 12:1)

Walter Lewis Wilson was a medical doctor who was deeply troubled about his ineffectiveness in sharing Christ with others. One day in 1913 a visiting missionary asked him a simple experiential question: "Who is the Holy Spirit to you?" Wilson took it for a theological inquiry, so his reply was this: "One of the Persons of the Godhead...Teacher, Guide, Third Person of the Trinity."

"You haven't answered my question," said his friend. Deflated, Wilson replied: "He is nothing to me. I have no contact with Him and could get along quite well without Him." Some time later Wilson was confronted with this thought from a gentleman named James Gray. "Have you noticed," said Gray, "that this verse (Romans 12:1) does not tell us to whom we should give our bodies. It is not the Lord Jesus. He has His own body. It is not the Father. He remains on His throne. Another has come to earth without a body. God gives you the honor of presenting your bodies to the Holy Spirit, to be His dwelling place on earth."

Wilson was moved. He cried out to God. "My Lord," he said, "I have treated You like a servant. When I wanted You, I called for You. Now I give You this body from my head to my feet. I give you my hands, my limbs, my eyes and lips, my brain. You may send this body to Africa, or lay it on a bed with cancer. It is your body from this moment on."

That prayer changed his life. Indeed, "With regard to my own experience with the Holy Spirit, the transformation in my life on January 14, 1914 was much greater than the change that took place when I was saved December 21, 1896."[19] Wilson went on to be a formidable lay evangelist, founded a church and Bible college, and authored over twenty books.

Questions: Whom do you know (contemporary or historically) whose whole life is/was possessed by the Holy Spirit? How do you know?

Prayer Request: Pray, if you are willing, something like Wilson's prayer above.

Day Thirty-Three

Week Five Memory Verse: Luke 4:18-19

Today's Verse: "Whether you turn to the right or to the left, your ears will hear a voice behind you, saying, 'This is the way; walk in it.'" (Isaiah 30:21)

One of the men I respect most in ministry once said that the "still, small voice" of the Spirit had never failed him. The guidance of God through the Spirit had always been there when he needed it most and the direction given had proven consistently true.

What he didn't tell people in the same moment was that he had practiced a 90-minute-a-day prayer habit for decades. A good bit of that daily time had been spent in listening to the Lord. Not speaking to Him. Not singing to Him. Not adoring or confessing or giving thanks or supplicating…but being quiet and listening.

After such a practiced commitment of heeding God's voice, I have no doubt that he was hearing the Spirit—not his own small voice whispering its desires, or anyone else's. Truth is, I believe the devil can provide a pretty persistent "small voice" when he wants to, and undoubtedly he has steered many a saint down a wrong path just that way.

So – how to discern the voice of the Spirit? Through a steady individual and corporate diet of the Word, of prayer, of fasting and of seeking godly counsel. But the old saint mentioned a moment ago had a point. We need to practice listening. And obeying when we think we have heard. And then reflecting as to whether we heard correctly. That is called, of course, practice.

When we try and succeed, we will learn the Voice. When we try and fail, that will instruct as well. But with all the voices out there vying for attention, it is good to have learned His and to develop a growing sensitivity to it. To do so will benefit us and the Kingdom in amazing ways.

Questions: Have you ever heard that "still, small voice?" How do you know? Have you ever thought you heard and didn't? Tell about that.

Prayer Request: Pray that God would help you to listen to Him. Today.

Day Thirty-Four

Week Five Memory Verse: Luke 4:18-19

Today's Verse: "Put on the full armor of God so that you can take your stand against the devil's schemes." (Philippians 6:11)

We have mentioned The Lausanne Covenant and its statement on the Spirit. The Lausanne Committee produced another document called The Manila Manifesto. In it, they said this:

> All evangelism involves spiritual warfare with the principalities and powers of evil, in which only spiritual weapons can prevail, especially the Word and the Spirit, with prayer. We therefore call on all Christian people to be diligent in their prayers both for the renewal of the church and for the evangelization of the world.

Spiritual war/weapons sounds a bit daunting. And yet, life in the Spirit is very much like that. C.S. Lewis put it this way in his formidable Mere Christianity:

> Enemy-occupied territory—that is what this world is. Christianity is the story of how the rightful king has landed, you might say landed in disguise, and is calling us all to take part in a great campaign of sabotage. When you go to church you are really listening in to the secret wireless from our friends: that is why the enemy is so anxious to prevent us from going....I know someone will ask me, "Do you really mean, at this time of day, to re-introduce our old friend the devil—hoofs and horns and all?" Well, what the time of day has to do with it I do not know. And I am not particular about the hoofs and horns. But in other respects my answer is "Yes, I do."[20]

Christians should love what is at their disposal – "the Word and the Spirit, with prayer." We need ample amounts of each! Specifically, we can pray for the renewal of the Church (another way of saying Holy Spirit revived Church) and for the evangelization of the nations.

Questions: Why would the Word, and the Spirit and prayer work so well against the devil and the powers of evil?

Prayer Request: Pray for more Word, Spirit and prayer in your church.

Day Thirty-Five

Week Five Memory Verse: Luke 4:18-19

Today's Verse: "But when he, the Spirit of truth, comes he will guide you into all truth." (John 16:13)

There are a thousand different ways that pastors try to present eternal truths of the Spirit in temporal containers so we might understand some of the mysteries of the Almighty. None, of course, is totally accurate; but taken as a whole many of these can help us fathom the truths of the Kingdom of God. James Merritt challenges our thinking with this comparison:

> There are hundreds of thousands of volts of energy available to your home and mine. But the only problem is, those volts sent in their own power would burn up our home. So knowing that, the engineers have built what is called transformers – not transmitters, but transformers. That transformer breaks down that electricity into meaningful units of power that you and I can use.

So, says Merritt, turn the corner and make an application to our listening to the Spirit:

> The Holy Spirit is God's transformer. He takes the incredible truth of God, and in the right place, at the right time, in the right way, gives it to us in such a way that we can handle it, and we can use it to give us the power that we need to be all that we need to be for God. Because He acts as the transformer of divine truth, we can receive it.[21]

Questions: Has the Spirit ever – in the right place, at the right time, in the right way – given you insight? Describe.

Prayer Request: Pray that God the Transformer will give you a lesson today in such a way that, although you might not have been able to receive it last night, or last week, or last year, you might receive it now.

Day Thirty-Six

Week Six Memory Verse: Romans 8:1-2 (see pg. 54)

Today's Verse: "In sacrifice and offering you have not delighted, but you have given me an open ear." (Psalm 40:6 ESV)

Harvard scholar Diana Eck, in her work entitled Encountering God (Boston: Beacon, 1993), revealed some fascinating special effects that the medieval church employed.[22] In the 10th century Roman church, for instance, cathedral ceilings contained strategically placed trap doors. They were called "Holy Spirit holes."

On Pentecost Sunday some brave souls would pull themselves up on the roof and, at the best liturgical moment, release live doves through these "Spirit holes." The choir would make sounds like a rushing wind and then, as if that weren't enough, with doves flying and wind blowing, bushel after bushel of rose petals were showered through the trap doors upon the crowd below, simulating the tongues of fire that came to rest on the gathered in Acts 2.

Diana Eck says our churches "need these Holy Spirit holes." She is right. Our churches need to be open to the Spirit and the wind and the tongues of fire. We need to be open to the mystery, the movement and the majesty of God. We need to be open to whatever surprises God wants to bring our way that dozens or hundreds or thousands of people – in one day! – might come to Him and be baptized.

Are our buildings too insulated? Our ceiling too closed off? Our expectations too low? Our minds too satisfied? Our doctrine too controlled?

Holy Spirit holes. In our lives, if not in our churches!

Questions: If we need to be more "open" to the Spirit what will that mean for us in a very practical sense?

Prayer Request: Pray we would be open to whatever the Spirit wants to do in our personal and corporate lives.

Day Thirty-Seven

Week Six Memory Verse: Romans 8:1-2

Today's Verse: "Blessed are those who hunger and thirst for righteousness, for they will be filled." (Matt. 5:6)

Sammy Morris was born in Liberia in the late 19th century. At the age of 14 his tribe was attacked and Sammy captured. Because he was a targeted prince, he was beaten severely. He miraculously escaped one night and fled to a coffee plantation. A missionary taught him what she knew, then directed him to the wealthy and well-connected Stephen Merritt of New York to satisfy Sammy's desire to know more about the Holy Spirit. Through several miracles and the enormous passion of Morris, he landed in New York and found Stephen Merritt.

Upon Sammy's arrival, Merritt took him on a carriage ride and began showing him the city sights—Central Park, Grand Opera House, the new bridge. Sammy asked, "Stephen Merritt, do you never pray in a coach?" Sammy knelt down and pulled Merritt down with him:

> Holy Ghost, I have come all the way from Africa to talk to Stephen Merritt about the Holy Ghost. Now I am here, he shows me the harbor, the churches, the banks and other things, but does not say one word about You. Take out of his heart the things of the earth, and so fill him with Yourself that he cannot speak or write or talk of anything but You.[23]

Sammy died just a few years later. Yet his hunger and passion for the Spirit changed Merritt's life and since then have inspired a dozen biographies, a film and a documentary, and five novels. Morris' dying wish was that many at his alma mater Taylor University and beyond would go to Africa because he would not be able to. His dream has been realized.

Questions: What do we desire more than the Holy Spirit? How might God bring a significant hunger for Him into our lives?

Prayer Request: Pray the Spirit would give you a passion for Himself, a hunger and a thirst that supersedes all other appetites.

Day Thirty-Eight

Week Six Memory Verse: Romans 8:1-2

Today's Verse: "Blessed are the merciful, for they will be shown mercy." (Matthew 5:7)

What happens when the Holy Spirit fills us? I remember hearing pastor Peter Lord explain it this way in a sermon at Asbury College - he invited one the students onstage and had him hold a glass of water. It was full, and the student, at the urging of Lord, promised not to spill the water. Lord then grabbed the student's arm and shook. Water, of course, went everywhere.

"What happened?" the student was asked. "You shook my arm!" said the young man. Wrong answer, said the preacher. Water didn't come out of the glass because his arm was shaken. Water came out of the glass because...there was water in the glass. And so the Chinese proverb goes: "Whatever you're filled to the brim with spills out when you are bumped." The Church, in its infancy and whenever it has been at its best, has always been bumped by political and cultural circumstances. When bumped, believers have often spilled out with God. And thus has the gospel travelled across the globe.

Rodney Stark, a sociologist of religion at Baylor University, says that Christianity grew quickly in the first several hundred years after Christ because they "outlived the pagans." By this he means that while pagan temples were having drinking bouts, Christians were serving the poor. When plagues hit the Empire they didn't run away, but to, the dying (sometimes at the cost of their own lives!). They treated women and their babies with dignity in the face of abuse and abortions. They provided charity and hope in overcrowded urban areas. When told to reject God they said "Jesus is Lord" and loved their persecutors.

When bumped, they spilled out with the Lord. It changed everything.

Questions: If Jesus spilled out of us today, what would happen?

Prayer Request: Pray to be filled. Pray for holy overflow when bumped.

Day Thirty-Nine

Week Six Memory Verse: Romans 8:1-2

Today's Verse: "And this is my prayer: that your love may abound more and more in knowledge and depth of insight, so that you may be...pure and blameless for the day of Christ..." (Philippians 1:9-10)

On the day of Pentecost Peter received the Holy Spirit. Years later, at the Council of Jerusalem, he had an opportunity to testify to the effect of that Holy Spirit on human lives, especially now that the Gentiles had begun receiving the same: "God, who knows the heart, showed that he accepted them, just as he did to us. He made no distinction between us and them, for he purified their hearts by faith."

Many, testifying concerning the Spirit, will talk about the power received. What impressed Peter in his memory of that day was purity. Both Jews and Gentiles were becoming free of sin and purified to be what God wanted them to be. A small sampling of verses along these themes:

- "Blessed are the **pure** in heart, for they will see God." (Mt. 5:8)
- "But now you have been **set free from sin**..." (Rom. 6:22)
- "Therefore there is now no condemnation for those who are in Christ Jesus because through Christ Jesus the law of the Spirit of life **set me free from the law of sin** and death..." (Rom. 8:1-2)
- "But I am afraid that just as Eve was deceived by the serpent's cunning, your minds may somehow be led astray from your sincere and **pure** devotion to Christ." (2 Cor. 11:13)
- "And this is my prayer: that your love may abound more and more in knowledge and depth of insight, so that you may be...**pure** and blameless for the day of Christ..." (Philippians 1:9-10)
- "Do not be hasty in the laying on of hands, and do not share in the sins of others. Keep yourself **pure**." (1 Tim. 5:22)
- "To him who loves us and has **freed us from our sins** by his blood..." (Rev. 1:5)

Questions: What in our lives needs to be purified? What sins does the Spirit need to set us free from? What does the Spirit need to do? What do we need to do?

Prayer Request: Pray that the Spirit might come in and purify our hearts and free us from ALL sin.

Day Forty

Week Six Memory Verse: Romans 8:1-2

Today's Verse: "And we all, who with unveiled faces contemplate the Lord's glory, are being transformed into his image with ever-increasing glory, which comes from the Lord, who is the Spirit." (2 Cor. 3:18)

The Holy Spirit transforms. The Lord changes us. He did it over and over in the Bible, and is still doing it today. Take Acts...[24]

- In the Gospels, Peter is a hothead and speaks before he thinks...in Acts, filled with the Spirit he stands and speaks on behalf of the Apostles.

- In 9:1 Saul is breathing out threats and murder; by 9:20 he is proclaiming Jesus as the Messiah in the synagogues.

- In 4:46 Barnabas is a rich, land-owning Levite. In the next verse he is giving his land away and is known as the 'Son of Encouragement.'

- In Mark 6:3 James is mentioned as a brother of Jesus and it is elsewhere noted that none of Jesus' brothers believed in Him. By Acts 15:13 he is the wise leader of the Jerusalem church who handles the most consequential Council in Christian history.

- In 10:1 Cornelius is a Roman solder and Godfearer. In 10:44 he is full of the Holy Spirit and getting baptized along with his family.

- In 6:5 Stephen is serving tables. In 7:51 he is a bold apologist who articulates the message of Christ so well Jesus is standing in heaven looking on.

- In 18:25 Apollos is an unbalanced teacher but by 18:28 is powerful and effective in his preaching and sent out from Ephesus to Greece.

- In 18:2 Priscilla and Aquila are dispirited refugees but by 18:26 they take Apollos into their house church and teach him about Christianity.

Questions: Has the Spirit done all the transforming He wants to do in you? What else needs to be done?

Prayer Request: Pray that the Spirit melts you, molds you, fills you, uses you.

Day Forty-One

Week Six Memory Verse: Romans 8:1-2

Today's Verse: "They broke bread in their homes and ate together with glad and sincere hearts." (Acts 2:46)

In Acts 2 they were "all together in one place" and were "filled with the Holy Spirit..." At the end of that chapter the growing Christian community could be found eating together and fellowshipping with one another in houses. Apparently, when the Holy Spirit is on the move some of His best work is done in homes.

- In Luke 8:39 Jesus told the demoniac to return to his house and talk about the things that had happened to him.
- In Luke 19:9 Jesus was eating with Zacchaeus in his home and said that salvation had come to his house.
- In John 4:53 the centurion's entire household believed.
- In Acts 10 Cornelius' entire household was baptized.
- In Acts 18:8 Crispus, the leader of the synagogue in Corinth, believed along with all his household.
- In Acts the church meets together in Jason's house (17:5), Justus's house (18:7), Philip's house (21:8).
- Sometimes it was for prayer (12:12), or an impromptu gathering (16:32) or for fellowship (20:7) or Communion ((2:46) or for an evangelistic report (28:17ff).

Says Michael Green: "The Acts give high priority to the home. It was the central pivot for the Christian advance....And the fact that they could not have had public meetings is beside the point. They would have gone for house meetings anyway, for the home is a priceless asset. It is informal and relaxed. It makes participation easy. The leader is not distant, but approachable.... Use them for Bible studies, for fellowship groups, for prayer meetings, for evangelistic outreach, for baptism groups, for anything." [25]

Questions: How could we better allow the Spirit to use our home? What ways might the Spirit use it even this week for evangelism and discipleship?

Prayer Request: Pray that God would use your home for Gospel advance.

Day Forty-Two

Week Six Memory Verse: Romans 8:1-2

Today's Verse: "And Peter said to them, 'Repent and be baptized every one of you in the name of Jesus Christ for the forgiveness of your sins, and you will receive the gift of the Holy Spirit.'" (Acts 2:38)

Blasio Kugosi was a schoolteacher in Rwanda, Central Africa, in 1935. He was discouraged by the lack of spiritual vitality in his church and, frankly, not pleased with his own experience in the Lord. He understood from the early Church that the way forward might be to get in a room alone for a week to fast and pray. That week changed him.

He came out convinced that he needed to confess his sins, particularly to those he had wronged. Among other things this meant humbly asking forgiveness from his wife and children. Thus freed from his past and cleansed in his heart he began to proclaim the gospel in the school where he taught. Revival broke out. Teachers and students found the Lord and they were soon called abaka – "people on fire."

Someone in the Anglican Church in Uganda heard about Blasio and asked him to come and share. He spoke directly to the leadership and the Spirit descended on that place with many, again, seeking the salvation of God. People were understandably encouraged about Blasio's ministry. Then, suddenly, he died of fever. His ministry of just a few weeks' duration was over.

But from those few engagements people took the message and spread it from person-to-person, village-to-village, nation-to-nation. What started with discouragement and fasting and prayer behind closed doors ended up in the mighty East African Revival. In the end, it wasn't a schoolteacher's ministry that was nearly as special as what the Spirit of God desired to do in Africa. Without a doubt, the fullness of God's Spirit had its impact.[26]

Questions: Do you feel at all dissatisfied with your relationship with the Lord? What should be done about it? Can Blasio's testimony help?

Prayer Request: Pray and fast for personal repentance and the Spirit's indwelling.

Day Forty-Three

Week Seven Memory Verse: Galatians 5:22-23 (see pg. 54)

Today's Verse: "When the Spirit of truth comes, he will guide you into all the truth, for he will not speak on his own authority, but whatever he hears he will speak, and he will declare to you the things that are to come." (John 16:13)

Years ago one of America's great evangelical leaders confessed his sin of adultery to Christianity Today. He described how the affair had come about and reported why he felt the need to confess publicly and resign his position in ministry. This quote was revealing: "Satan's ability to distort the heart and the mind is beyond belief. I assume the responsibility for what I did; I made those decisions out of a distorted heart."[27] The leader was eventually restored to ministry and today helps others in healing from similar situations.

Satan is without doubt a distorter or, in the words of one favorite biblical scholar, "a confuser." In contrast the Spirit is the great Clarifier. He brings understanding and discernment to our hearts and minds. So, when the fullness of the Clarifier was invited back into this evangelical leader's life, he was restored. Clarifier replaced Confuser!

Gary Cockerill, a professorial colleague of mine, once preached a chapel message at our seminary using the metaphor of an eye chart. Eye charts have a series of letters which the examinee attempts to identify or an "E" pointing in various directions. But, said Dr. Cockerill, imagine an eye chart with a cross on it. The disciples, lacking the proper focus, keep looking at the chart and offering seemingly absurd interpretations: "I see a throne," says one. "An easy chair!" says someone else. "An Oval Office!" But they never see the cross…the suffering…the shame…the pain. They needed the Clarifier.

He came. The disciples accurately perceived the message. And they carried their Crosses to the ends of the world.

Questions: Where in your life do you need clarification? How could the Spirit help?

Prayer Request: Pray for the work of the Spirit of Clarity, even in areas where you don't yet know that you need it.

Day Forty-Four

Week Seven Memory Verse: Galatians 5:22-23

Today's Verse: "See, I have chosen Bezalel...and I have filled him with the Spirit of God, with skill, ability and knowledge in all kinds of crafts..." (Ex. 31:2-3)

When the Spirit fills He is frequently getting us ready for a work. In Exodus (31:1-11, 35:30-36:7) we read about Bezalel "filled with the Spirit of God" – the first instance of such an infilling in the Bible. A few phrases later he is described as being "filled with skill." The reason? The Tabernacle awaited construction and it was going to take more than a simple laborer to complete the task of building the very dwelling place of God. Interestingly, God brings in others equipped by Him to help Bezalel. Money to complete the job came in abundance as well.

None of these details should be overlooked. Whether the task at hand is the construction of a holy place or carrying the gospel to the ends of the earth God fills people with Himself and bids them go. Typically, others God equips for a similar vision are linked to the project. His mission will never lack the resources necessary for final accomplishment, whether material or personnel.

The point is that God wants to fill you with Himself to accomplish His will. Too many think that the infilling of the Spirit is primarily for an exuberant personal experience and rarely imagine that God has a task and is preparing them to do it. There are things the Spirit wants to do in us, to be sure; but our outward-bound God wants to engage us in the glorious work of the Great Commission.

Enjoy Him. But also embrace the work He has for you to do.

Questions: What task in the Kingdom is the Spirit talking to you about these days? What role does God want you to play in the Great Commission?

Prayer Request: Pray that the Spirit would reveal what skills He wants to use to accomplish His will through your life.

Day Forty-Five

Week Seven Memory Verse: Galatians 5:22-23

Today's Verse: "Blessed are the poor in spirit, for theirs I the kingdom of heaven." (Mt. 5:3)

The Spirit is a Christ-like Spirit, a Holy Spirit. Therefore the Spirit's work in us will produce character that reflects Jesus. There are no better words to describe this character than the beatitudes of the Sermon on the Mount, where Jesus brushes a self-portrait of his own nature.

- Jesus said blessed are the **poor in spirit**. Philippians 2:7ff says that Jesus left the prerogatives of heaven and "made himself nothing." This is known as the great kenosis passage (from the Greek word for emptiness) which refers to the self-emptying of ourselves that we might be filled with God's will. Blessing, Jesus says, comes with emulating His kenosis in our spirits. On the other side of Pentecost we can recognize this as the emptying of our spirit for the fullness of His Spirit.

- Jesus said blessed are **those who mourn**. We should have our hearts broken over the things that break the heart of God. First and foremost we must weep over our own sins that not only cause God grave disappointment but moved Christ to die on the cross. Beyond that, we look at sin's effect in the world, and the Spirit tenderizes our sensibilities to issues like abortion, sex-trafficking, crime, hunger, poverty, homelessness, disease, etc. We mourn and then find God moving us from tears to action.

    In 1912, General William Booth of the Salvation Army gave his last address to 7,000 Salvationists in London. His final words: "While women weep, as they do now, I'll fight; while children go hungry, as they do now I'll fight; while men go to prison, in and out, in and out, as they do now, I'll fight; while there is a poor lost girl upon the streets, while there remains one dark soul without the light of God, I'll fight, I'll fight to the very end!" He died three months later.

Questions: What would it mean for you to be increasingly empty of yourself? What does God want you to mourn over in the world?

Prayer Request: Pray for emptiness, and then fullness. Pray your heart would be broken over the things that break God's heart.

Day Forty-Six

Week Seven Memory Verse: Galatians 5:22-23

Today's Verse: "Blessed are the meek, for they will inherit the earth." (Mt. 5:5)

The beatitudes reflect the character of Christ. He seems to be saying, This is what I am, this is what I want you to be.

- Jesus said blessed are **the meek.** In the days of Jesus "meek" was a term used for horses. A horse might be wild at some point, but once captured, tamed and trained he would be under control of the master, useable for the purposes of man. As Jesus was absolutely under the control of the Father, so He desired we be under the Spirit's control for the purposes of God. Gentle, easily guided, obedient, desirous to please.

- Jesus said blessed are those who **hunger and thirst for righteousness**. When we become like Christ our appetites change. Once we might have had a voracious hunger, even an addiction, for food or sports or money or sex or drugs or alcohol. Paul writes to the church at Ephesus: "Do not get drunk on wine…Instead, be filled with the Spirit (Eph. 5:18). And when you get full of the Spirit, you tend to want more. E. Stanley Jones was once asked at a school assembly if there was anything he didn't have that he wanted. No, he said, I only want more of what I already have.

- Jesus said blessed are **the merciful.** Barclay says that the Greek word here means to get inside the other person's skin in order to see from their perspective, to feel with their insight and experience.[28] Henri Nouwen writes in The Wounded Healer about "the willingness to move to the aid of other people and to make the fruits of our own woundedness available to others." The best healers are those who have been, and indeed are, wounded. They know about about pain, about inconvenience, about loneliness, about ostracism. And, thus, they compassionately move toward those who know the same.

Questions: Of these three characteristics of Jesus, which is a strength of someone you know? How can the Spirit help strengthen that in your life?

Prayer Request: Pray that you might be meek, hungry/thirsty, merciful.

Day Forty-Seven

Week Seven Memory Verse: Galatians 5:22-23

Today's Verse: "Seek first His kingdom and His righteousness, and all these things will be given to you as well." (Mt. 6:33)

To be like Jesus means to reflect His beatitudes—what John Wesley called the "sum of all true religion in eight particulars."[29] Today we look at one of these marks of Christ.

Jesus said blessed are the **pure in heart**. "As a very little dust will disorder a clock," said John Wesley, "and the least sand will obscure our sight, so the least grain of sin which is upon the heart will hinder its right motion toward God."[30] Cleanliness of our hearts is vital for holy progress!

I used to have a problem with Mt, 6:33: "Seek first the Kingdom…" Too open-ended in my mind – put the King in spot #1, then add whatever you want second, third, fourth, etc. It didn't seem congruent with the radical call of the New Testament. So I looked up the word for first in the Greek (proton) in the Theological Dictionary of the New Testament. This is what it had to say: "The meaning (in Mt. 6:33) cannot be that one must first seek after God's kingdom and then after other things. 'Above all' is the only meaning which corresponds to the central position which orientation to the kingdom of God has in the proclamation of Jesus. Indeed, proton is so exclusive here that it carries the implication of 'only.'"[31] Now that made sense! If we were to make an outline it might look like this:

   I.   The King
        a. Church
        b. Family
        c. Business
        d. Et cetera.

But there is no Roman numeral "II."

Questions: Soren Kierkegaard said "Purity of heart is to will one thing." What is that "one thing" of your life? Is it the right thing?

Prayer Request: Pray to the Spirit for the "only" brand of purity.

Day Forty-Eight

Week Seven Memory Verse: Galatians 5:22-23

Today's Verse: "Peace I leave with you; my peace I give you." (Jn. 14:27)

We continue our study of the life of Jesus found in the beatitudes...

- Jesus said blessed are **the peacemakers**. War, of course, is terrible. But He meant something more than just the absence of conflict among nations or warring parties. He desired *shalom*, which meant completeness, soundness, wellness, peace, contentment and friendship among people but especially with God in covenant relationship. But Jesus wants more. He wants us to *make* peace. This can happen in a thousand ways, but one of the best is to see our role as bridges of God to sinful men. Most people come to know Christ through relationships, these "bridges". As we strengthen our relationships with the unchurched we find the Spirit walking right over that love of our friendships into the lives of people who don't know Him. We thus begin to fulfill our mandate to be peacemakers, shalom bridges.

- Jesus said blessed are those **persecuted for the sake of righteousness.** People transformed by the Spirit are bold for their faith by, among other things, being courageous evangelistic peacemakers. But this can unnerve those not touched yet by Christ. And for centuries this has meant the shedding of blood, the loss of life. William Barclay says, "There are three characteristics that marked the NT Christian. First, they were absurdly happy. Second, they were filled with an irrational love for their enemies. Third, they were always in trouble."[32] Indeed, it was said of Paul, "We have found this man to be a troublemaker, stirring up riots among the Jews all over the world." (Acts 24:5) "For the sake of righteousness" can mean difficulties, and the Spirit-filled meet that trouble, by God's grace, with glad rejoicing.

Questions: Where in your church or community does God need you to help make shalom? When persecution comes, how will the Spirit sustain you?

Prayer Request: Pray the Spirit makes us shalom-makers. Pray for the persecuted Church around the world.

Day Forty-Nine

Week Seven Memory Verse: Galatians 5:22-23

Today's Verse: "I will make breath enter you, and you will come to life." (Ez. 37:5)

Edwin Hatch was a formidable scholar in the late nineteenth century. He taught at Oxford University and was somewhat famous for sophisticated addresses known as the Brampton Lectures which were translated into German by the world renowned Adolph von Harnack. He produced some other notable works including a concordance of the Septuagint (Greek translation of the Old Testament), still in use today.

Scholar, Oxford, Brampton Lectures, expert on the Septuagint. Yet this intellectual was also a poet. In 1878 he wrote an unforgettable hymn.

> Breathe on me, breath of God,
> Fill me with life anew,
> That I may love what Thou dost love,
> And do what Thou wouldst do.
>
> Breathe on me, breath of God,
> Until my heart is pure,
> Until with Thee I will one will,
> To do and to endure.
>
> Breathe on me, breath of God,
> Till I am wholly Thine,
> Until this earthly part of me
> Glows with Thy fire divine.
>
> Breathe on me, breath of God,
> So shall I never die,
> But live with Thee the perfect life
> Of Thine eternity.

Ruach and the Greek pneuma were frequently translated both breath and Spirit. The breath of God is His Spirit.

Questions: What thought captivates you the most: fill me with life anew...until my heart is pure...till I am wholly Thine...so shall I never die? Why?

Prayer Request: Pray that hymn, line by line.

Day Fifty

Week Seven Memory Verse: Galatians 5:22-23

Today's Verses: "From the day after the Sabbath, the day you brought the sheaf of the wave offering, **count off seven full weeks. Count off fifty days** up to the day after the seventh Sabbath, and then present an offering of new grain to the LORD... On that same day you are to proclaim a sacred assembly and do no regular work. This is to be a lasting ordinance for the generations to come, wherever you live. When you reap the harvest of your land, do not reap to the very edges of your field or gather the gleanings of your harvest. Leave them for the poor and for the foreigner residing among you. I am the LORD your God.'" (Lev. 23:15-16, 21)

"When the day of Pentecost came, they were all together in one place. Suddenly a sound like the blowing of a violent wind came from heaven and filled the whole house where they were sitting. They saw what seemed to be tongues of fire that separated and came to rest on each of them. All of them were filled with the Holy Spirit and began to speak in other tongues as the Spirit enabled them." (Acts 2:1-4)

There are four major holidays in the Christian year:

- Christmas
- Good Friday
- Easter
- Pentecost

Most churches don't do much with the last one. But we should. Shavu'ot, or the Feast of Weeks (7 weeks leading up to Pentecost from the Passover) is what the Jews call it. It commemorated the time when the first fruits were harvested and brought to the Temple as well as the giving of the Torah at Mount Sinai. For Christians it meant the day when the Spirit came upon the believers and birthed the Church. It was also the day when these Old Testament verses came alive with fresh meaning:

> "The days are coming," declares the LORD, "when I will make a new covenant with the people of Israel and with the people of Judah. It will not be like the covenant I made with their ancestors when I took them by the hand to lead them out of Egypt,

because they broke my covenant, though I was a husband to them," declares the LORD. "This is the covenant I will make with the people of Israel after that time," declares the LORD. "I will put my law in their minds and write it on their hearts. I will be their God, and they will be my people. No longer will they teach their neighbor, or say to one another, 'Know the LORD,' because they will all know me, from the least of them to the greatest," declares the LORD. "For I will forgive their wickedness and will remember their sins no more." (Jeremiah 31:31-34)

"I will sprinkle clean water on you, and you will be clean; I will cleanse you from all your impurities and from all your idols. I will give you a new heart and put a new spirit in you; I will remove from you your heart of stone and give you a heart of flesh. And I will put my Spirit in you and move you to follow my decrees and be careful to keep my laws." (Ezekiel 36:25-27)

The fifty days counting up to Pentecost should be days of great anticipation. It draws the connection between Jesus and the Spirit and the Word. Indeed, it is still customary for some Jews to stay up the entire first night of Shavu'ot and study Torah, then pray as early as possible in the morning.

These should be days of great anticipation because the Spirit of Jesus wants to work His life-transforming miracles again and again and again. He wants to fill, mold, use, spread. If we don't anticipate it can happen again, it probably won't. If we do, here it comes.

Further, Pentecost should be a party for Christians because it is our birthday. It is a celebration of the Spirit. It is the day of great harvest – 3,000 new Christians on the first Pentecost after the resurrection of Jesus. It is the day when we celebrate the foregoing verses of Jeremiah and Ezekiel coming alive in our lives like never before.

<blockquote>
Spirit of faith, come down,
reveal the things of God,
and make to us the Godhead known,
and witness with the blood.
'Tis thine the blood to apply
and give us eyes to see,
who did for every sinner die
hath surely died for me.
</blockquote>

> Inspire the living faith
> (which whosoe'er receive,
> the witness in themselves they have
> and consciously believe),
> the faith that conquers all,
> and doth the mountain move,
> and saves whoe'er on Jesus call,
> and perfects them in love.[33]

Questions: What kind of harvest has God done in your own spirit through this 50-day study of the Holy Spirit? What does He want to do in you and through you in days ahead?

Prayer: Pray over the answers you just answered. Pray through the hymn.

Memory Verses

Scripture memory is a powerful discipleship tool. Dallas Willard, professor and author, said that

> "Bible memorization is absolutely fundamental to spiritual formation. If I had to choose between all the disciplines of the spiritual life, I would choose Bible memorization, because it is a fundamental way of filling our minds with what it needs. This book of the law shall not depart out of your mouth. That's where you need it! How does it get in your mouth? Memorization."[34]

Memory work can be done either privately or in a group. Since this devotional might be used quite a bit in a group, here are some tips:

- The leader should initially read a small portion of the passage and then, as the portion is read again, participants should try to say the verse with the leader. In unison! As best you can! Indeed, sometimes you must mumble along best as you can!

- Start with a sentence. Add a sentence the next day. Repeat two or three times. Add another sentence the next day. Repeat.

- After the passage is memorized thoroughly (along with the verse number) repeat all that has been memorized each setting before new memory work is begun.

- Mealtime is a good time for memory work (particularly if you eat together at least daily). If not, choose another time (perhaps bedtime?) where this devotional guide and discussion, prayer and memory work can be accomplished.

- When these verses have been memorized, keep going. Memorizing the rest of your life will take your Christian walk far.

Memory should accomplish the following, and much more!

- Strengthen your mind for God.
- Increasingly give you the mind of Christ.
- Give you holy words to meditate on whenever you have a few moments of quiet.
- Give you a great foundation for communication with God.
- Give you confidence in your daily walk and boldness for your next challenge.

The Weekly Verses for "50 Days"

Week One: "Go therefore and make disciples of all nations, baptizing them in the name of the Father and of the Son and of the Holy Spirit, teaching them to observe all that I have commanded you. And behold, I am with you always, to the end of the age." (Mt. 28:19-20)

Week Two: "Now the Lord is the Spirit, and where the Spirit of the Lord is, there is freedom." (2 Corinthians 3:17)

Week Three: "If you love me, keep my commands. And I will ask the Father, and he will give you another advocate to help you and be with you forever—the Spirit of truth. The world cannot accept him, because it neither sees him nor knows him. But you know him, for he lives with you and will be in you." (John 14:15-17)

Week Four: "I will give you a new heart and put a new spirit in you; I will remove from you your heart of stone and give you a heart of flesh. And I will put my Spirit in you and move you to follow my decrees and be careful to keep my laws." (Ezekiel 36:26-27)

Week Five: "The Spirit of the Lord is on me, because he has anointed me to proclaim good news to the poor. He has sent me to proclaim freedom for the prisoners and recovery of sight for the blind, to set the oppressed free, to proclaim the year of the Lord's favor." (Luke 4:18-19)

Week Six: "Therefore, there is now no condemnation for those who are in Christ Jesus, because through Christ Jesus the law of the Spirit who gives life has set you free from the law of sin and death." (Romans 8:1-2)

Week Seven: "But the fruit of the Spirit is love, joy, peace, patience, kindness, goodness, faithfulness, gentleness, self-control; against such things there is no law." (Galatians 5:22-23)

Footnotes

[1] E. Stanley Jones, Conversion, (New York: Abingdon Press, 1959), 231-232.

[2] E. Stanley Jones, Christ of Every Road, (New York: The Abingdon Press, 1930), 47.

[3] E. Stanley Jones, Ibid, 94.

[4] Craig Keener, The Bible Background Commentary: New Testament, (Downers Grove: InterVarsity Press, 1993), pg. 80.

[5] Clarence Jordan, The Substance of Faith, (New York: Association Press, 1972), pg. 13.

[6] John Stott, The Message of Acts, (Downers Grove: IVP Academic, 1994), pgs. 88-95

[7] John Calvin, Calvin's New Testament Commentaries: Acts Vol. 1. http://www.ccel.org/ccel/calvin/calcom36.html

[8] Garrison Keillor, "My Five Most Important Books," in the "Life in Books" section of Newsweek Magazine (12-24-07), 17

[9] Adapted from James Emery White, Long Night's Journey into Day (WaterBrook, 2002).

[10] John Walton, et. al., The Bible Background Commentary: Old Testament, (Downers Grove: InterVarsity Press, 2000), 28.

[11] John Wesley, Sermon CXLI: The Holy Spirit. http://wesley.nnu.edu/john-wesley/the-sermons-of-john-wesley-1872-edition/sermon-141-on-the-holy-spirit/

[12] John Pollock, Moody: A Biographical Portrait (Grand Rapids: Zondervan, 1963) 99.

[13] John Wesley, 52 Standard Sermons: Sermon 7 – "The Way to the Kingdom" (Salem: Schmul Publishing Co., 1982) 64.

[14] Several sources on the internet. Editor's notes.

[15] E. Stanley Jones, Christ of Every Road, (New York: The Abingdon Press, 1930), 69.

[16] Richard Foster, Freedom of Simplicity, (Harper & Row, 1981), 185.

[17] Donald B. Strobe, "The Shy Member of the Trinity", sermons.com

[18] The Athanasian Creed.

[19] Robert Morgan, On This Day Devotional: 365 Amazing and Inspiring Stories about Saints Martyrs & Heroes (Nashville: Thomas Nelson Publishers, 1997), "January 14."

[20] C.S. Lewis, Mere Christianity (New York: MacMillan Publishing Co., Inc., 1952) 45-46.

[21] James Merritt, "God's Guidance System", sermons.com

[22] taken from Leonard Sweet, "Holy Spirit Holes", sermons.com

[23] W. Terry Whalin, Samuel Morris, (Uhrichsville, Ohio: Barbour Publishing, 1999), 106.

[24] taken from Michael Green, 30 Years That Changed the World, (Grand Rapids: Eerdmans Publishing, 1993), 70-71.

[25] Michael Green, Ibid, 117. Also, examples from Charles Arn, et. al. Growth: A New Vision for the Sunday School, Church Growth Press, 73-74.

[26] Ajith Fernando, The NIV Application Commentary: Acts (Grand Rapids: Zondervan, 1998), 118.

[27] "A Talk with the MacDonald's," Christianity Today, July 10, 1987, 38.

[28] William Barclay, The Gospel of Matthew, Vol. 1 (Philadelphia: The Westminster Press, 1958), 98.

[29] John Wesley, 52 Standard Sermons, (Salem: Schmul Publishing Co., 1982) 206.

[30] John Wesley, A Plain Account of Christian Perfection (Kansas City: Beacon Hill Press, 1966) 110.

[31] Editors Gerhard Kittel/Gerhard Friedrich, Theological Dictionary of the New Teatament, (Grand Rapids: Erdmann's Publishing), Vol. 6, pg. 870.

[32] William Barclay, author's personal files.

[33] Charles Wesley, "Spirit of Faith, Come Down" verses 1, 4, (1746).

[34] Dallas Willard, "Spiritual Formation in Christ for the Whole Life and Whole Person" in Vocatio, Vol. 12, no. 2, Spring, 2001, p. 7.

Made in the USA
Middletown, DE
28 March 2018